GUITAR STANDARDS

TRANSCRIBER CREDITS

JESSE GRESS

ALL OF YOU
EASTER PARADE
HOW INSENSITIVE (INSENSATEZ)
I REMEMBER YOU
I'LL REMEMBER APRIL
LOVER MAN (OH, WHERE CAN YOU BE?)
MISTY
MOONLIGHT IN VERMONT
SATIN DOLL
SEVEN COME ELEVEN
SOFTLY AS IN A MORNING SUNRISE
SONG FOR MY FATHER
THE WAY YOU LOOK TONIGHT

JACK GRASSEL

ALL THE THINGS YOU ARE
TANGERINE
WHEN SUNNY GETS BLUE

ISBN 0-634-00034-9

HAL•LEONARD®
CORPORATION

7777 W. BLUEMOUND RD. P.O. BOX 13819 MILWAUKEE, WI 53213

For all works contained herein:
Unauthorized copying, arranging, adapting, recording or public performance is an infringement of copyright.
Infringers are liable under the law.

Visit Hal Leonard Online at
www.halleonard.com

GUITAR STANDARDS

CONTENTS

DISCOGRAPHY

ALL OF YOU	KENNY BURRELL: *KENNY BURRELL* PRESTIGE OJCCD-019-2 (P-7088)
ALL THE THINGS YOU ARE	HANK GARLAND: *JAZZ WINDS FROM A NEW DIRECTION* COLUMBIA JCS8372
EASTER PARADE	HERB ELLIS & RAY BROWN: *SOFT SHOE* CONCORD JAZZ CCD-6003
HOW INSENSITIVE (INSENSATEZ)	PAT MARTINO: *FOOTPRINTS* 32 JAZZ 32021
I REMEMBER YOU	TAL FARLOW: *JAZZ MASTERS* 41 VERVE 314 527 365-2
I'LL REMEMBER APRIL	GRANT GREEN: *STANDARDS* BLUE NOTE CDP 7243 8 21 21284 2 7
LOVER MAN (OH, WHERE CAN YOU BE?)	DJANGO REINHARDT: *DJANGOLOGY 49* BLUEBIRD 9988-2-RB
MISTY	BARNEY KESSEL/SHELLY MANNE/ RAY BROWN: *THE POLL WINNERS EXPLORING THE SCENE* CONTEMPORARY OJCCD-969-2 (57581)
MOONLIGHT IN VERMONT	JOHNNY SMITH QUINTET: *MOONLIGHT IN VERMONT* EMD/CAPITOL (ROOST 2211)
SATIN DOLL	JOE PASS: *PORTRAITS OF DUKE ELLINGTON* PABLO PACD-2310-716-2
SEVEN COME ELEVEN	CHARLIE CHRISTIAN: *THE GENIUS OF THE ELECTRIC GUITAR* COLUMBIA CK 40846
SOFTLY AS IN A MORNING SUNRISE	JIM HALL/RON CARTER DUO: *ALONG TOGETHER* MILESTONE OJCCD-467-2 (M-9045)
SONG FOR MY FATHER	GEORGE BENSON: *COMPACT JAZZ* VERVE 833 292-2
TANGERINE	JIMMY RANEY: *THE MASTER* CRISS CROSS JAZZ 1009
THE WAY YOU LOOK TONIGHT	WES MONTGOMERY TRIO: *WES MONTGOMERY ON THE GO* RIVERSIDE OJCCD-489-2 (RLP-9494)
WHEN SUNNY GETS BLUE	GEORGE BARNES: *BLUES GOING UP* CONCORD CJ-43

The *Classic Jazz Masters Series* is a collection of folios that contain some of the finest improvised performances ever recorded. Well-known master jazz players are represented, as well as gifted performers who are not commonly transcribed and published in jazz folios.

The performances transcribed in this book span 38 years. We carefully selected sixteen guitarists who we feel best represent the golden age of jazz guitar's development. Then, we searched for the finest example of each guitarist interpreting the works of a song in the standard jazz repertoire. Special effort was also made to include performances in a variety of settings: solo, duo, trio, quartet, and even larger ensembles.

We hope you will enjoy and learn from these great jazz masters.

—The Editors

FOREWORD

All of You

Words and Music by Cole Porter

* Tempo fluctuates between 54 - 84 b.p.m.

Copyright © 1954 by Cole Porter
Copyright Renewed, Assigned to Robert H. Montgomery, Trustee of the Cole Porter Musical and Literary Property Trusts
Chappell & Co. owner of publication and allied rights throughout the world
International Copyright Secured   All Rights Reserved

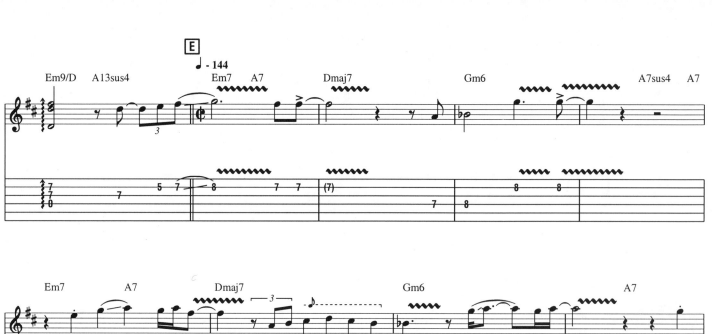

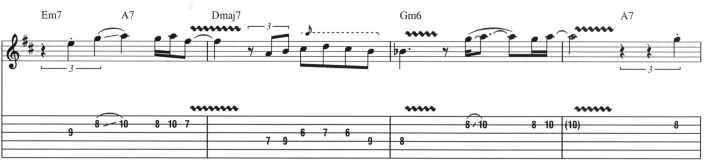

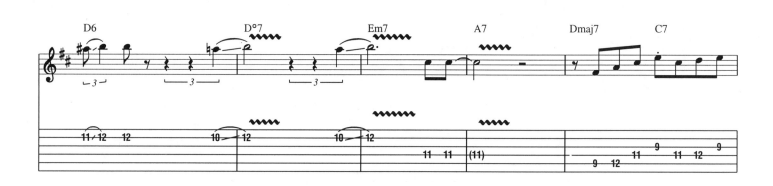

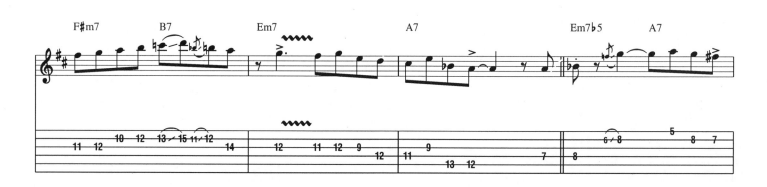

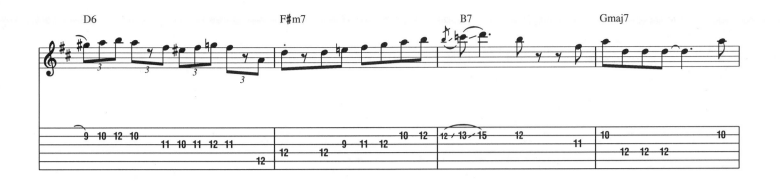

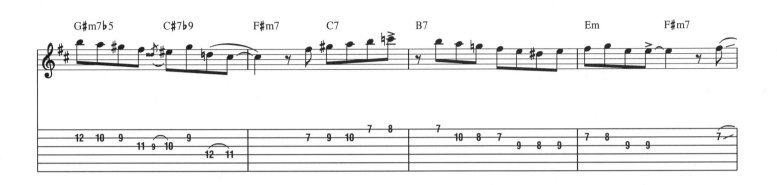

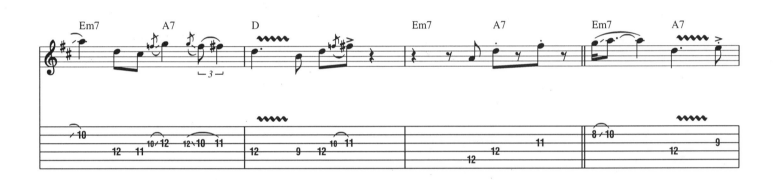

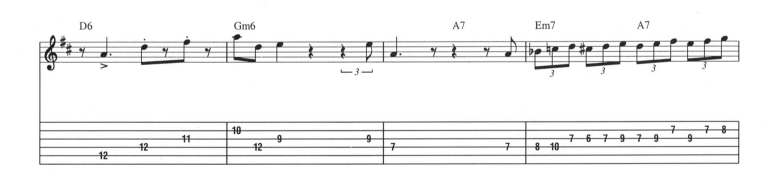

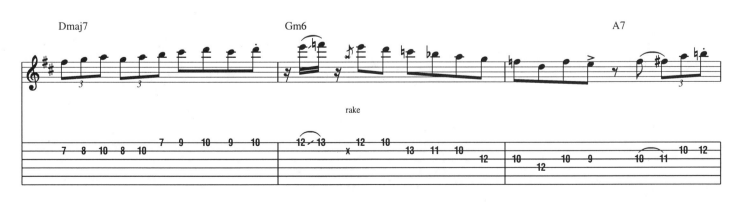

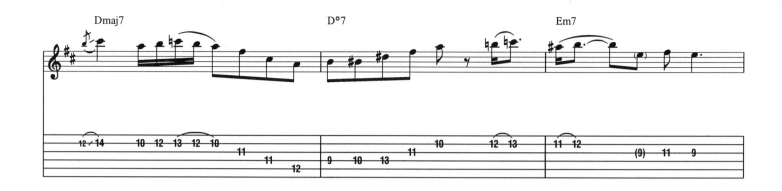

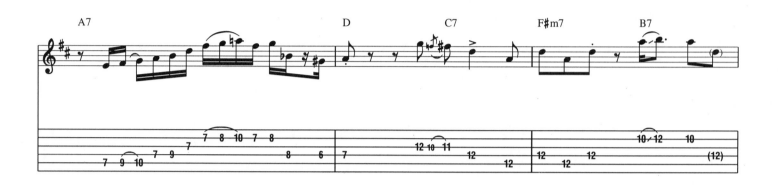

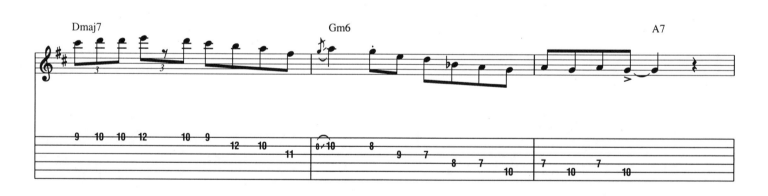

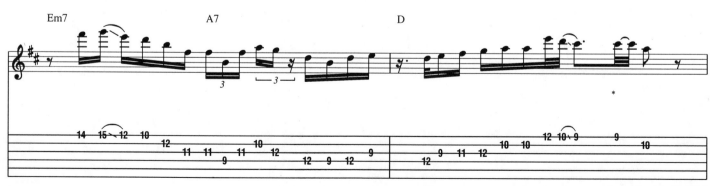

* note unintentionally pulled
off fretboard to sound F♯.

All the Things You Are

from VERY WARM FOR MAY

Lyrics by Oscar Hammerstein II
Music by Jerome Kern

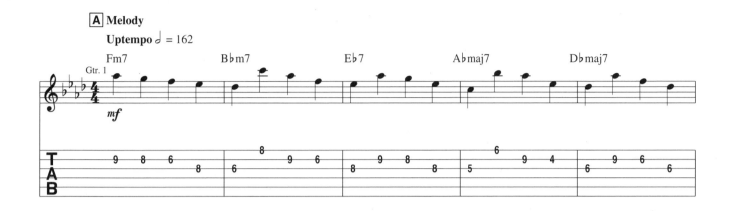

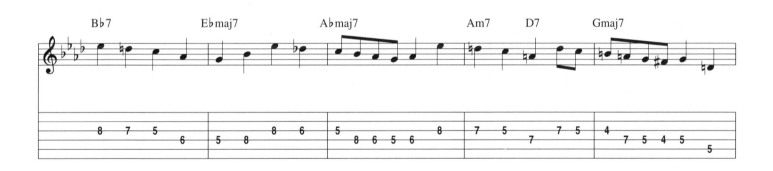

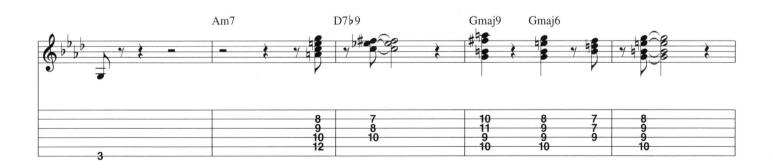

© 1939 UNIVERSAL - POLYGRAM INTERNATIONAL PUBLISHING, INC.
Copyright Renewed
This arrangement © 1996 UNIVERSAL - POLYGRAM INTERNATIONAL PUBLISHING, INC.
International Copyright Secured   All Rights Reserved

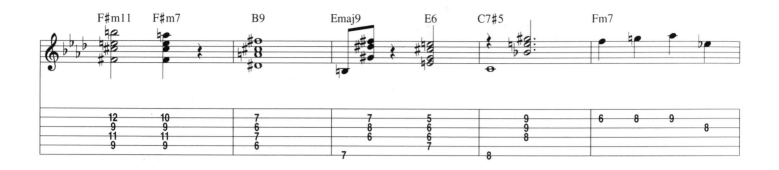

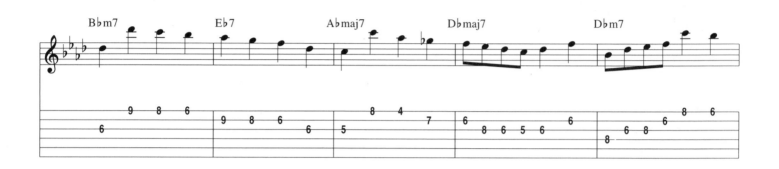

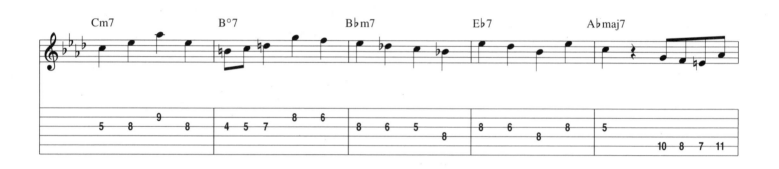

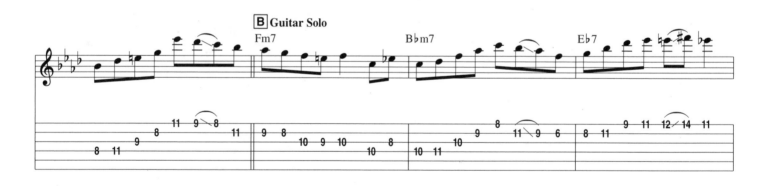

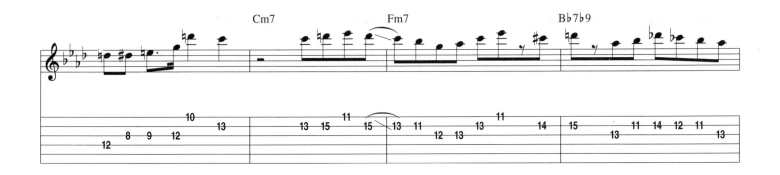

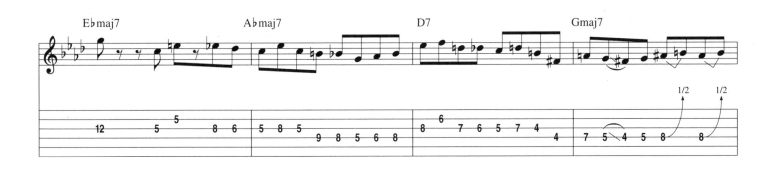

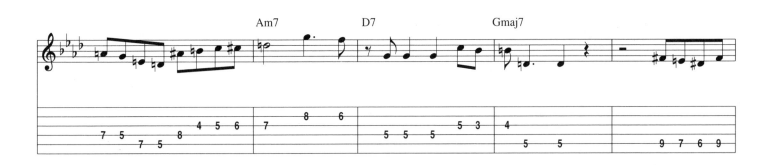

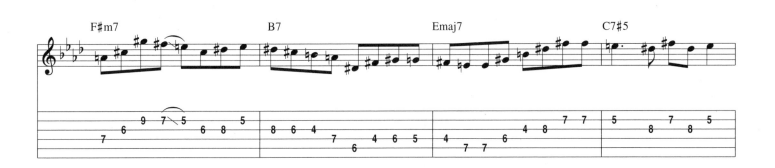

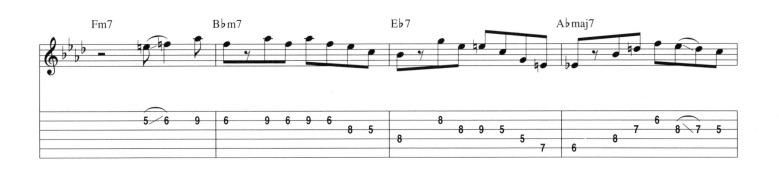

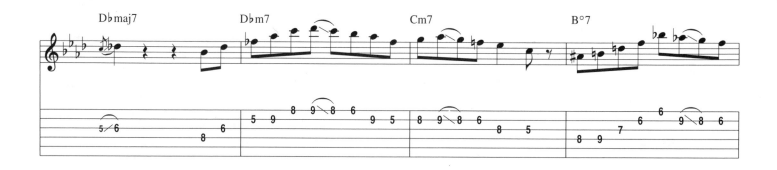

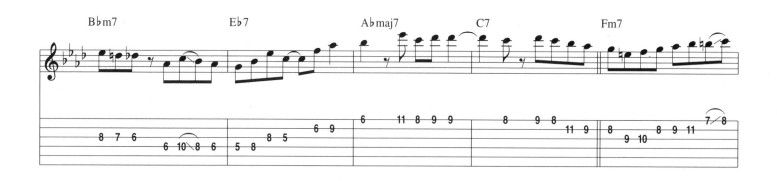

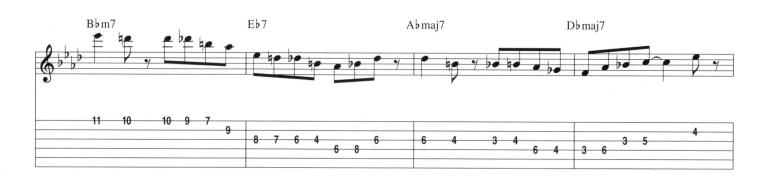

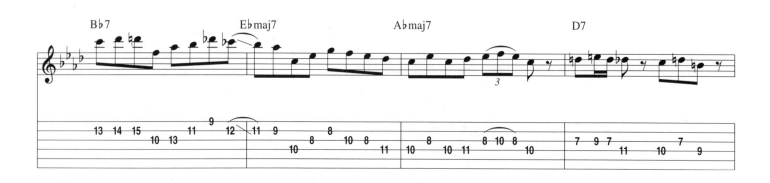

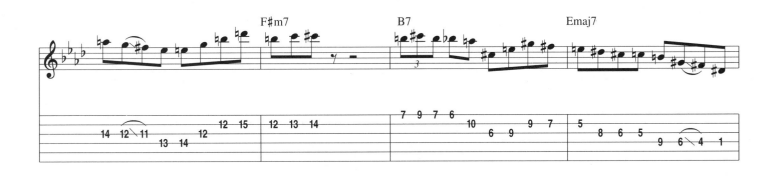

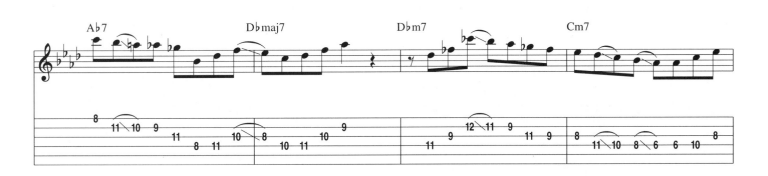

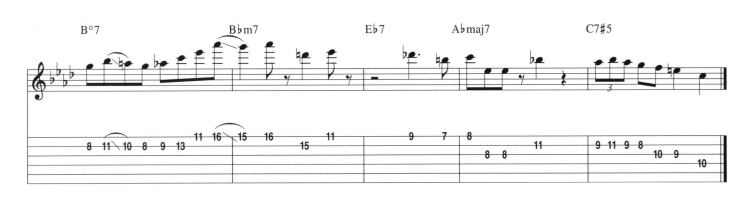

featured in the Motion Picture Irving Berlin's EASTER PARADE

Easter Parade

Words and Music by Irving Berlin

* Tempo fluctuates between 62-84 b.p.m.

© Copyright 1933 by Irving Berlin
Copyright Renewed
International Copyright Secured   All Rights Reserved

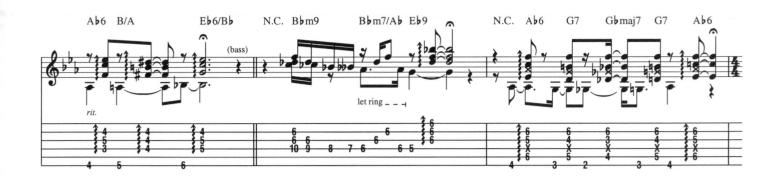

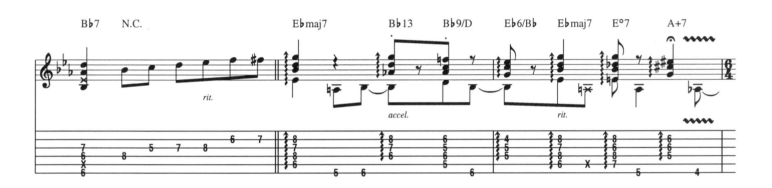

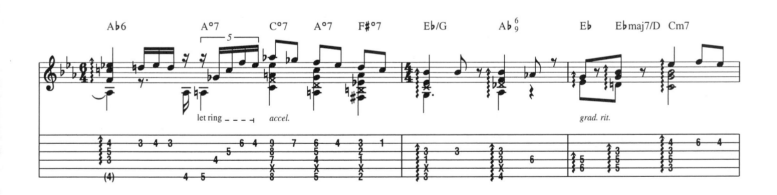

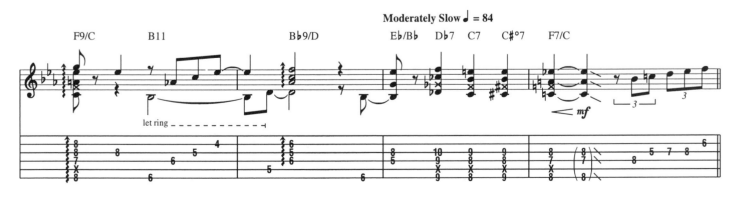

* Played behind the beat.

How Insensitive (Insensatez)

Music by Antonio Carlos Jobim
Original Words by Vinicius de Moraes

* Played behind the beat.

© 1963, 1964 UNIVERSAL - DUCHESS MUSIC CORPORATION
Copyright Renewed
This arrangement © 2000 UNIVERSAL - DUCHESS MUSIC CORPORATION
All Rights Reserved   Used by Permission

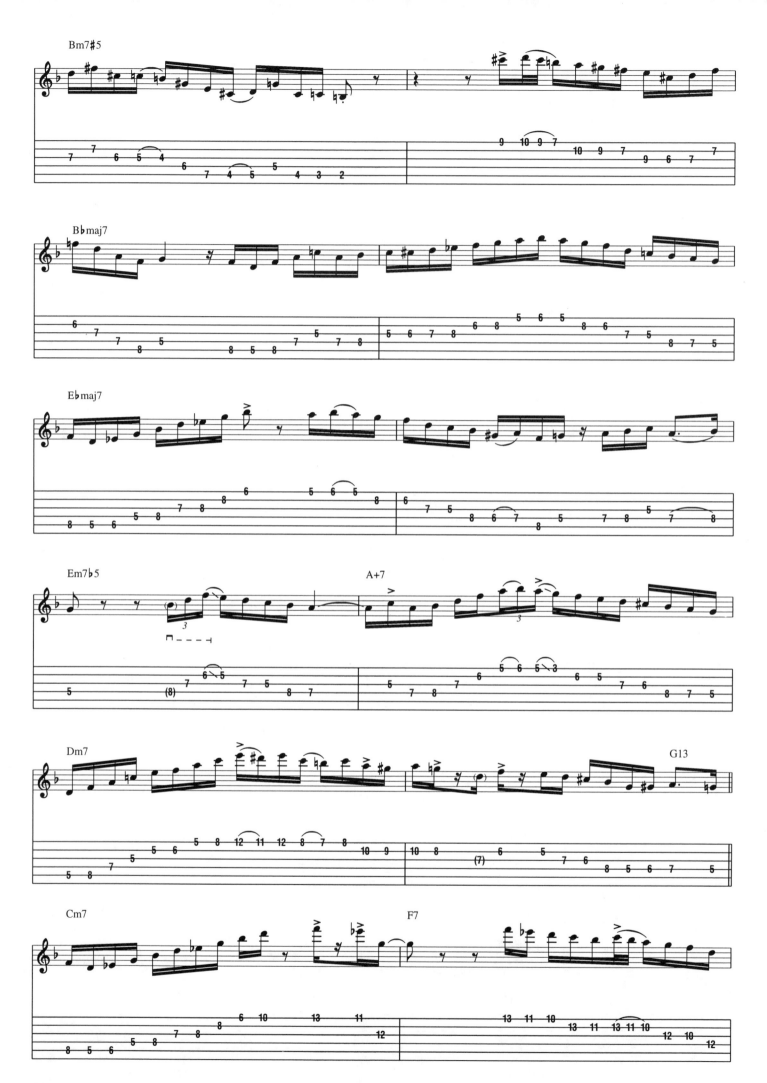

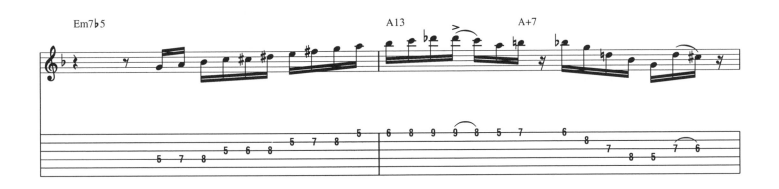

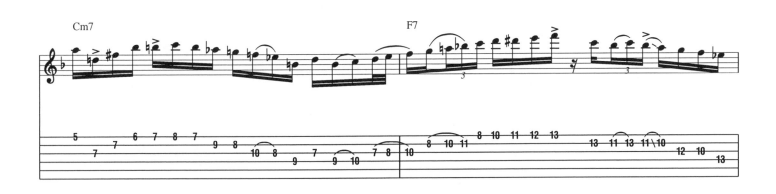

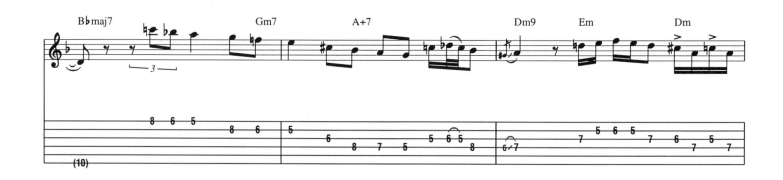

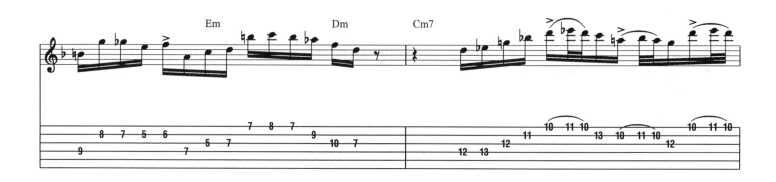

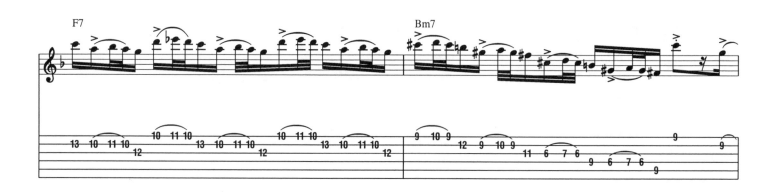

from the Paramount Picture THE FLEET'S IN

I Remember You

Words by Johnny Mercer
Music by Victor Schertzinger

Copyright © 1942 (Renewed 1969) by Paramount Music Corporation
International Copyright Secured   All Rights Reserved

* Played as even eighth notes.

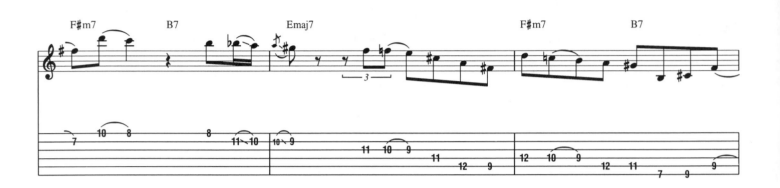

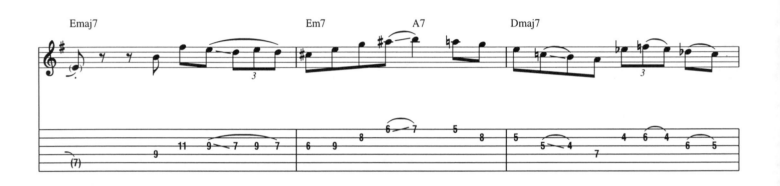

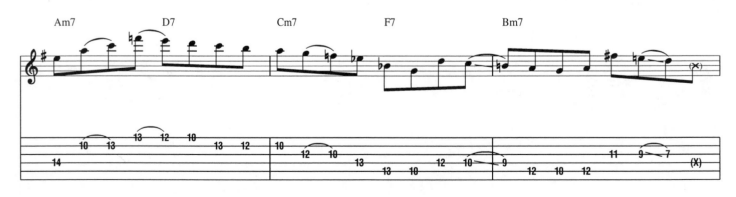

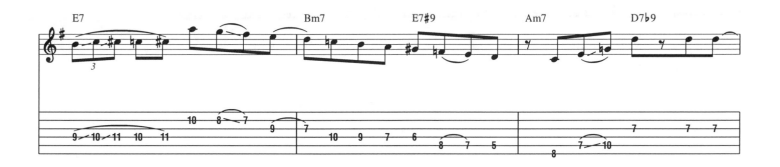

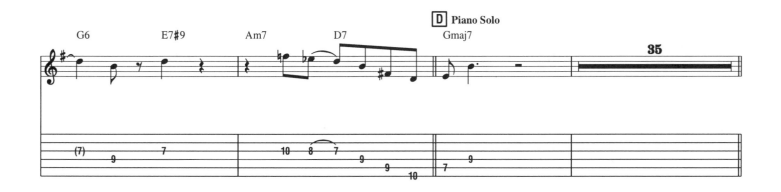

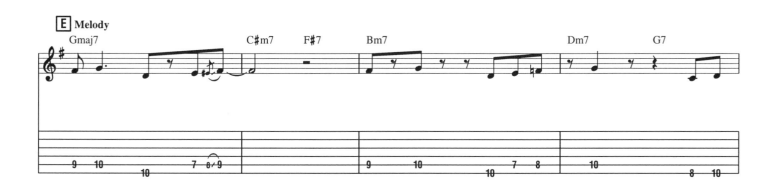

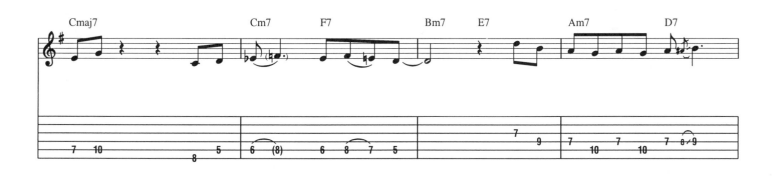

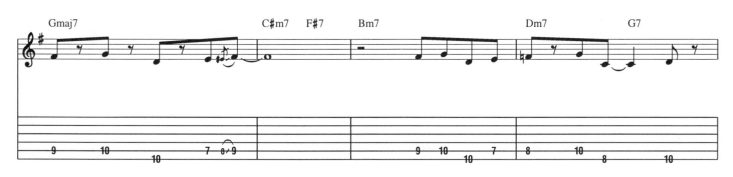

I'll Remember April

Words and Music by Pat Johnson, Don Raye, and Gene De Paul

© 1941, 1942 (Renewed) PIC CORPORATION and UNIVERSAL - MCA MUSIC PUBLISHING, A Division of UNIVERSAL STUDIOS, INC.
All Rights Reserved

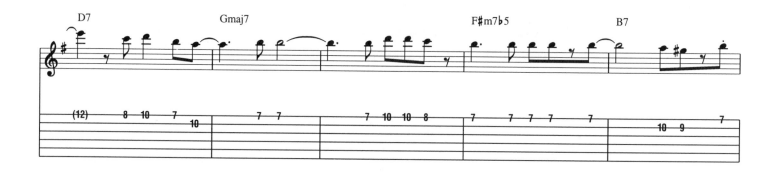

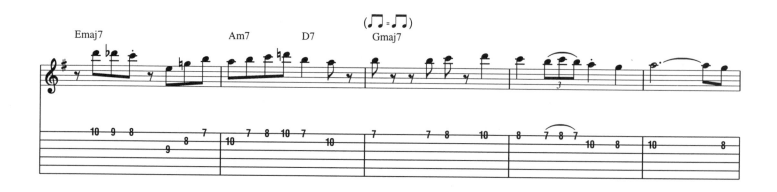

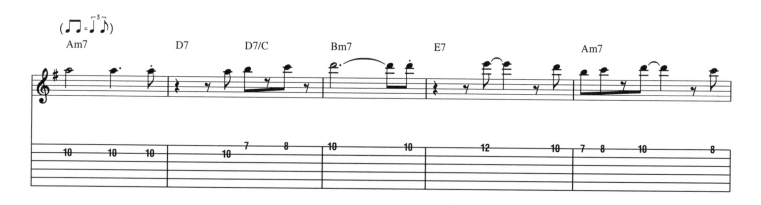

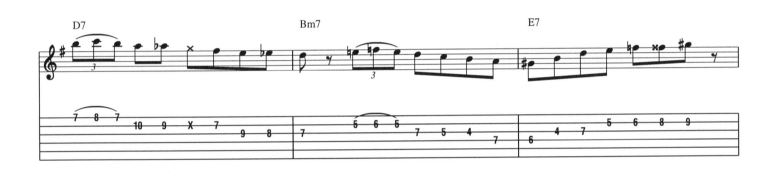

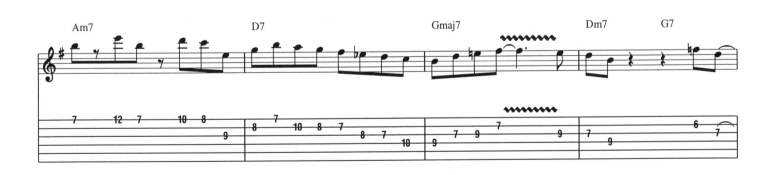

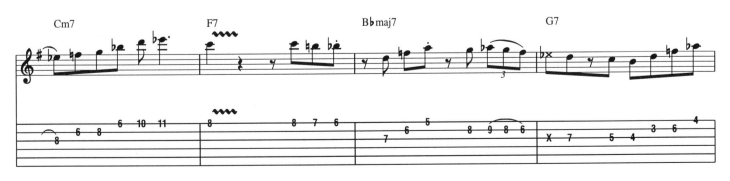

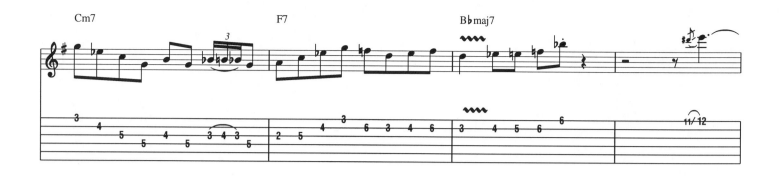

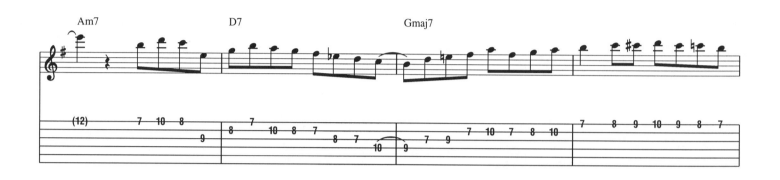

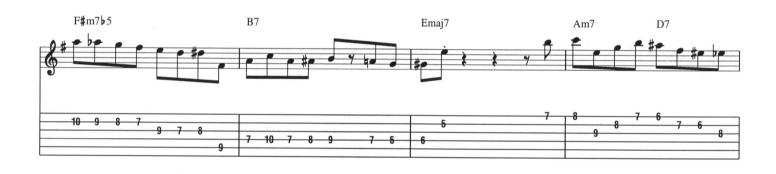

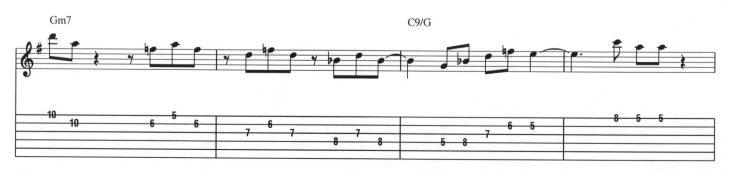

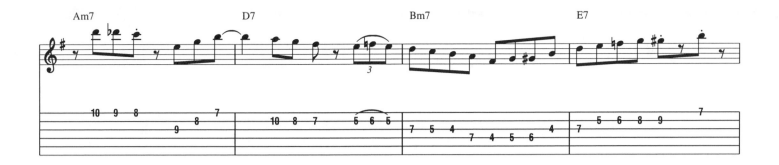

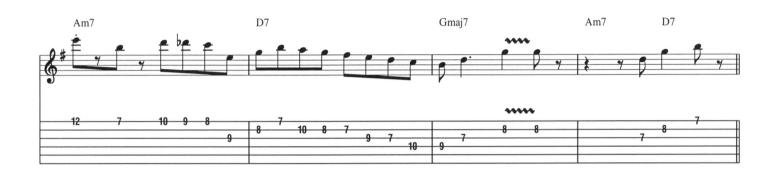

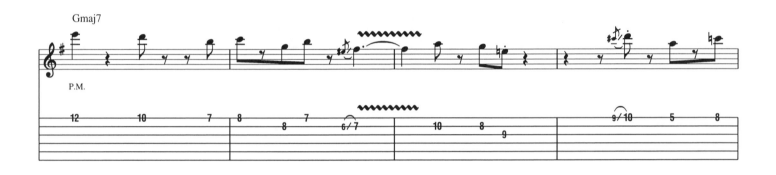

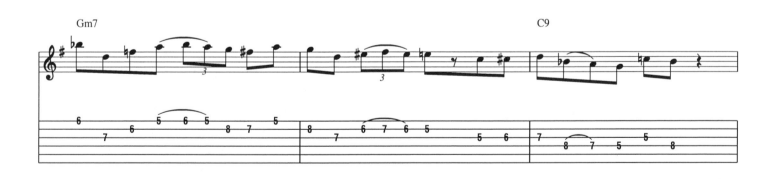

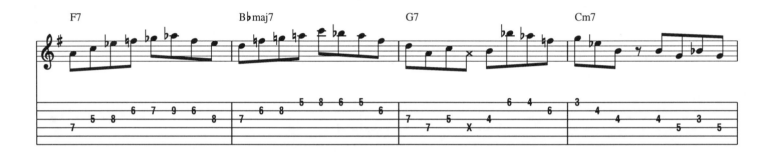

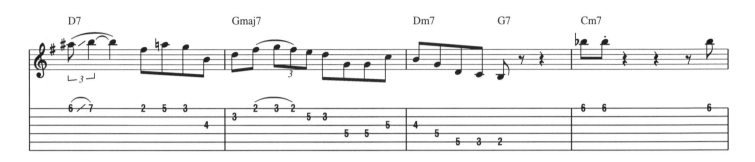

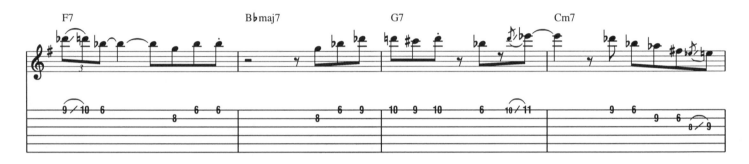

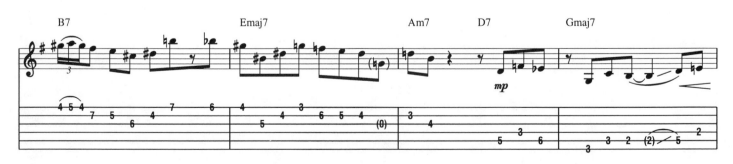

* Gtr. and drums exchange 4 meas. solos ("trade fours") throughout section.

Lover Man (Oh, Where Can You Be?)

By Jimmy Davis, Roger "Ram" Ramirez and Jimmy Sherman

*Played behind the beat.

© 1941, 1942 UNIVERSAL - MCA MUSIC PUBLISHING, A Division of UNIVERSAL STUDIOS, INC.
Copyright Renewed
This arrangement © 2000 UNIVERSAL - MCA MUSIC PUBLISHING, A Division of UNIVERSAL STUDIOS, INC.
All Rights Reserved   Used by Permission

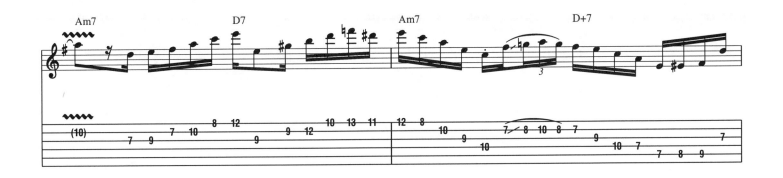

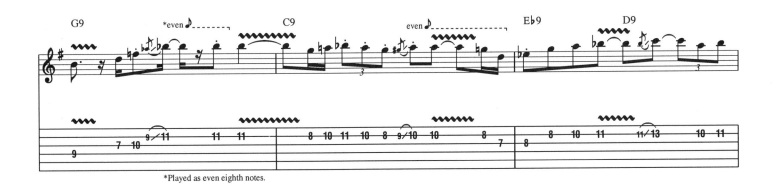

*Played as even eighth notes.

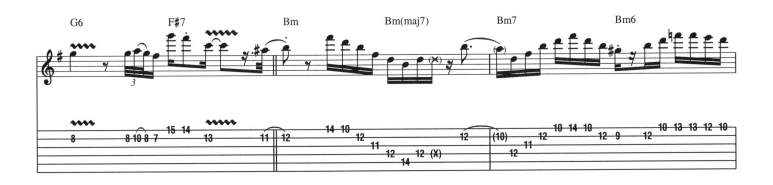

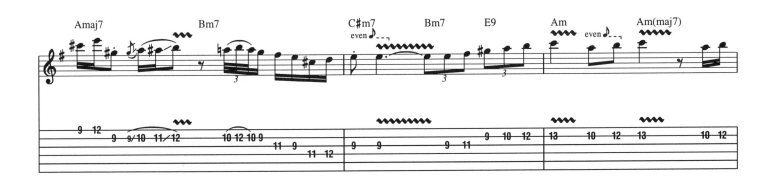

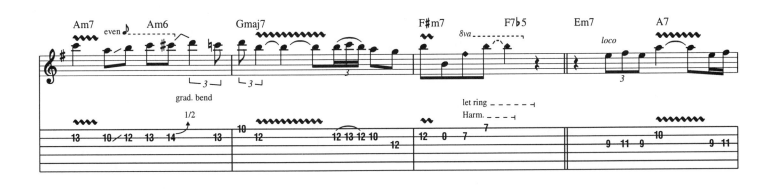

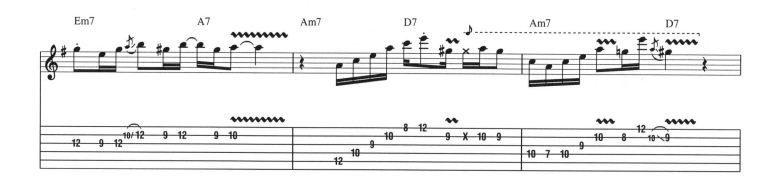

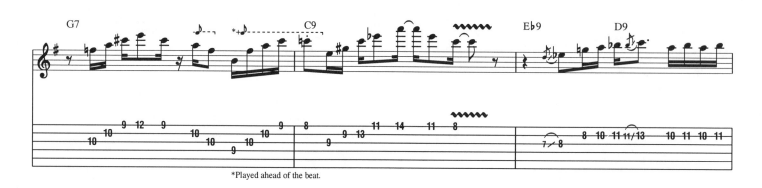

*Played ahead of the beat.

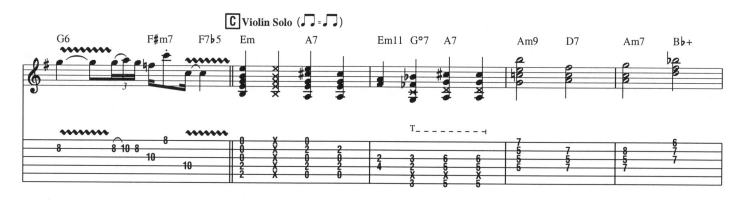

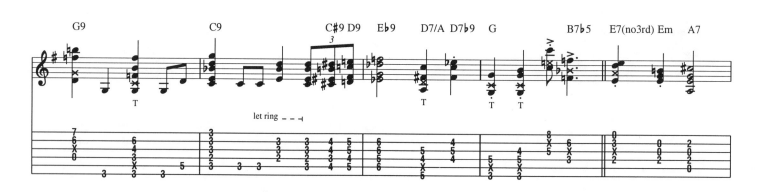

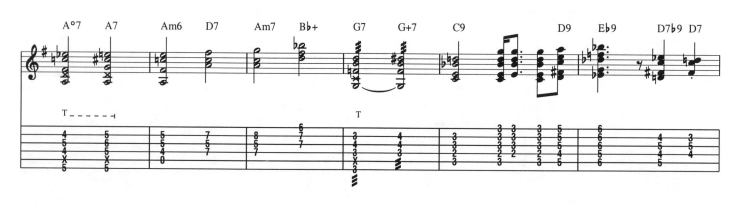

Misty

Music by Erroll Garner

Copyright © 1955 by Octave Music Publishing Corp.
Copyright Renewed
International Copyright Secured   All Rights Reserved

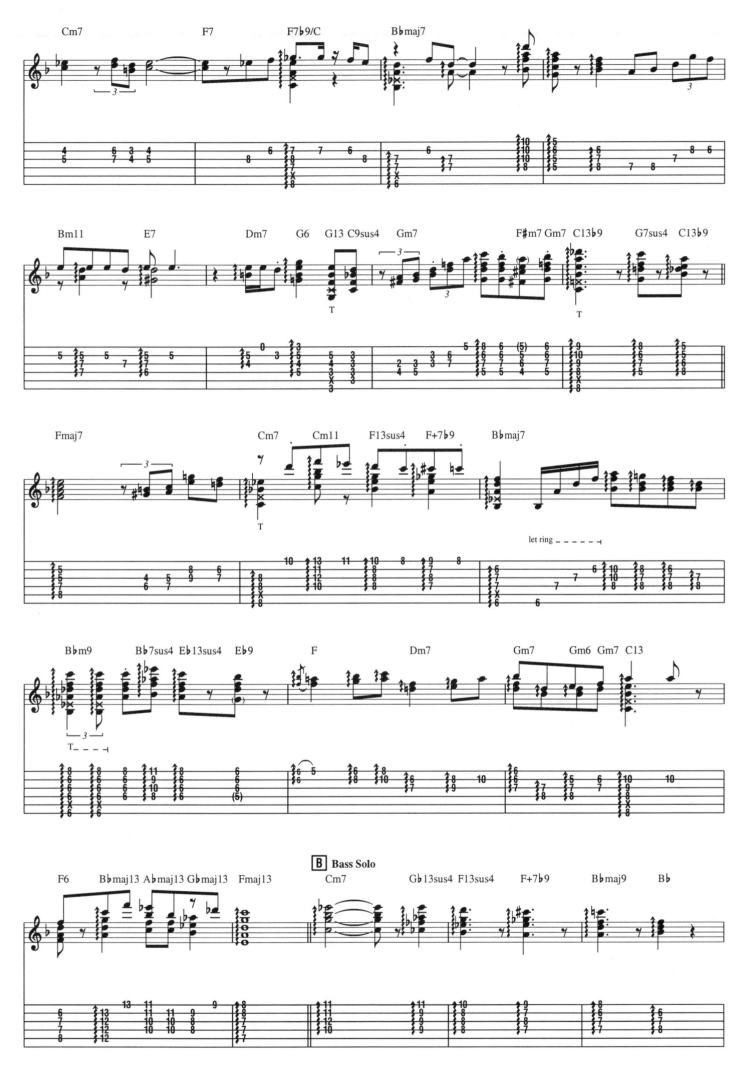

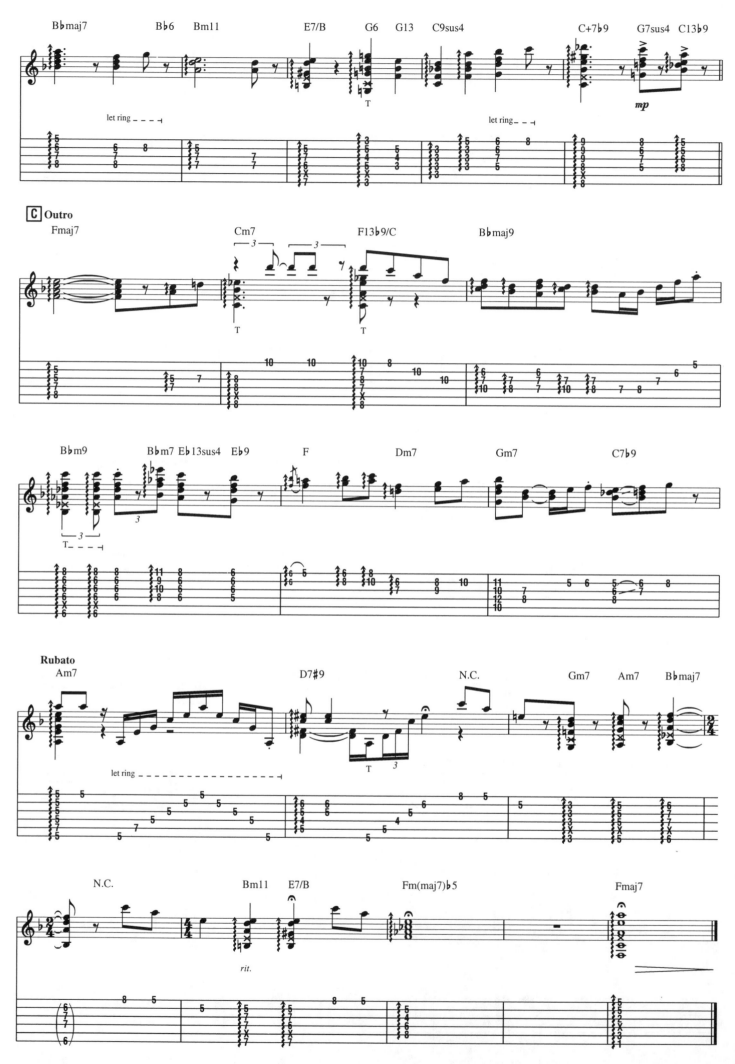

Moonlight in Vermont

Words and Music by John Blackburn and Karl Suessdorf

* Chord symbols reflect implied tonality.

Copyright © 1944 (Renewed 1972) Michael H. Goldsen, Inc.
International Copyright Secured   All Rights Reserved

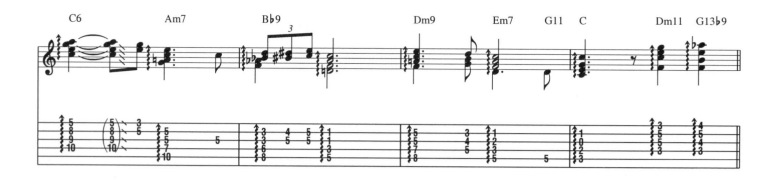

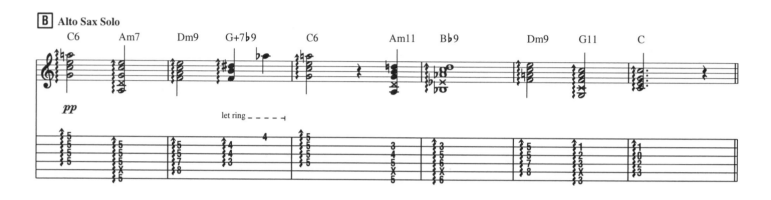

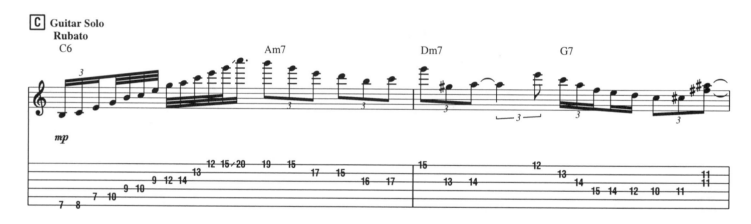

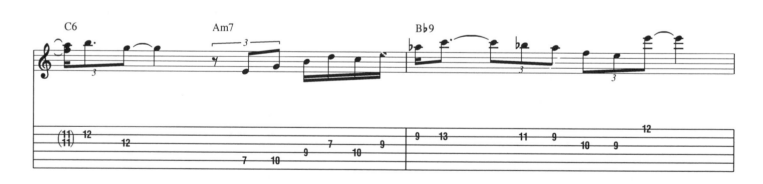

Satin Doll
from SOPHISTICATED LADIES

By Duke Ellington

Copyright © 1953 (Renewed 1981) and Assigned to Famous Music Corporation in the U.S.A.
Rights for the world outside the U.S.A. Controlled by Tempo Music, Inc. c/o Music Sales Corporation
International Copyright Secured   All Rights Reserved

*Played behind the beat.

Seven Come Eleven

By Benny Goodman and Charlie Christian

Copyright © 1940 by Regent Music Corporation
Copyright Renewed by Ragbag Music Publishing Corporation and Regent Music Publishing Corporation
All Rights for Ragbag Music Publishing Corporation Controlled and Administered by Jewel Music Publishing Co., Inc.
International Copyright Secured   All Rights Reserved
Used by Permission

Softly As in a Morning Sunrise

Lyric by Oscar Hammerstein II
Music by Sigmund Romberg

*Chord symbols reflect implied tonality.

Copyright © 1928 by Bambalina Music Publishing Co. and Warner Bros. Inc. in the United States
Copyright Renewed
All Rights on behalf of Bambalina Music Publishing Co. Administered by Williamson Music
International Copyright Secured   All Rights Reserved

*Gtr. and bass exchange eight meas. solos throughout section.

*Pat strings w/ palm of picking hand in specified rhythm.

Song for My Father

By Horace Silver

© 1964, 1966, 1969, 1987 by Ecaroh Music, Inc.
Copyright Renewed 1992
International Copyright Secured   All Rights Reserved

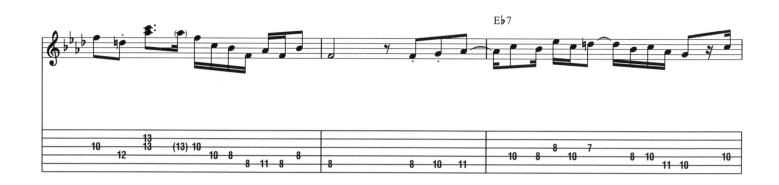

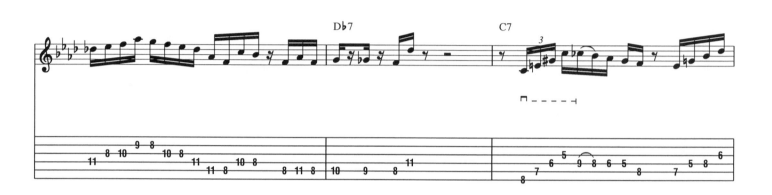

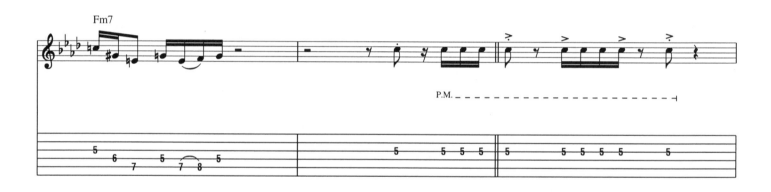

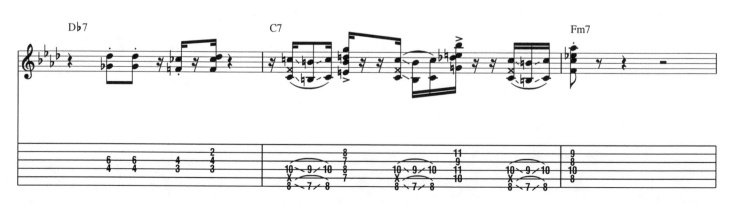

Tangerine

from the Paramount Picture THE FLEET'S IN

Words by Johnny Mercer
Music by Victor Schertzinger

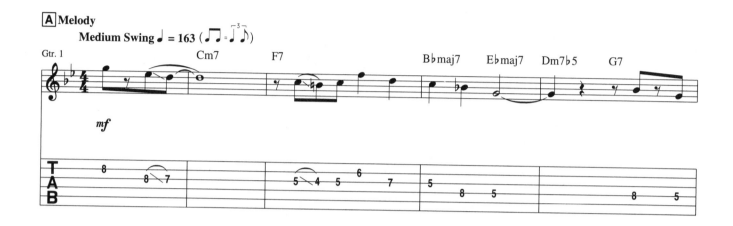

Copyright © 1942 (Renewed 1969) by Famous Music Corporation
International Copyright Secured   All Rights Reserved

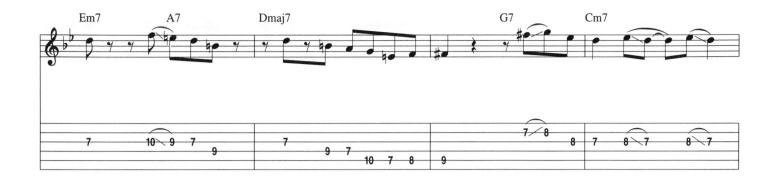

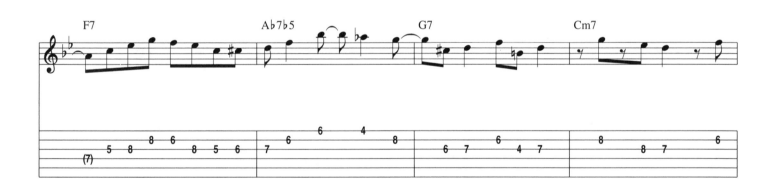

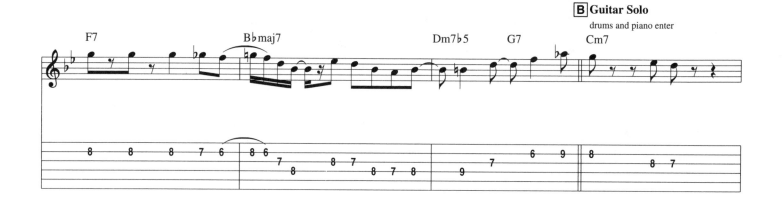

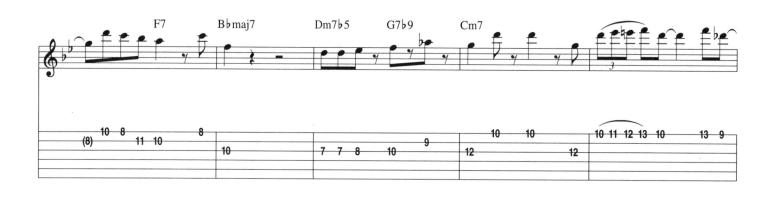

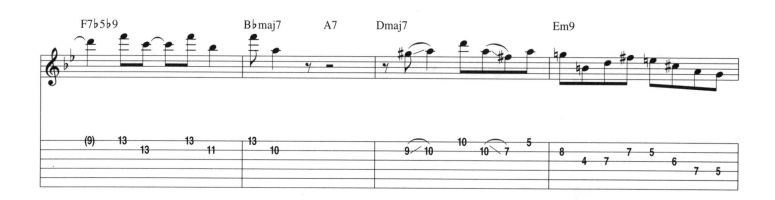

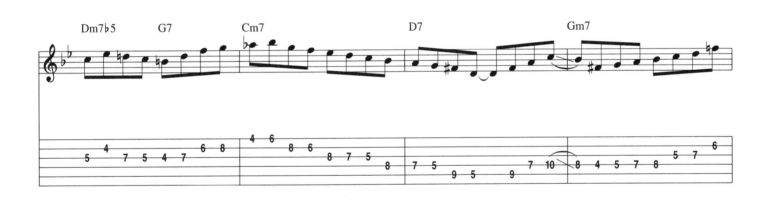

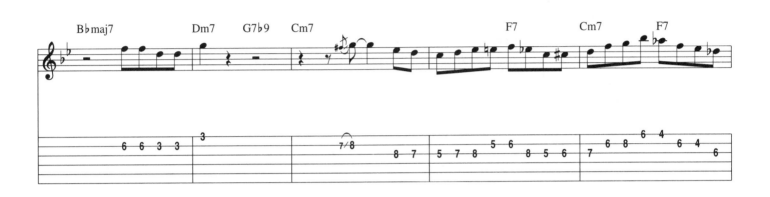

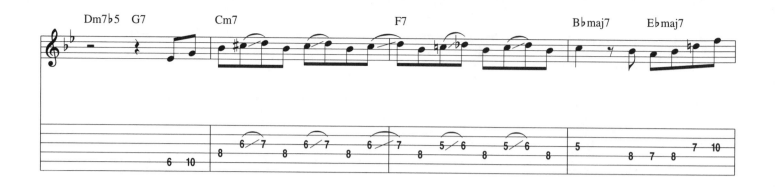

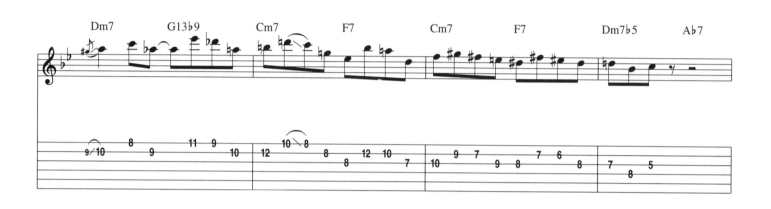

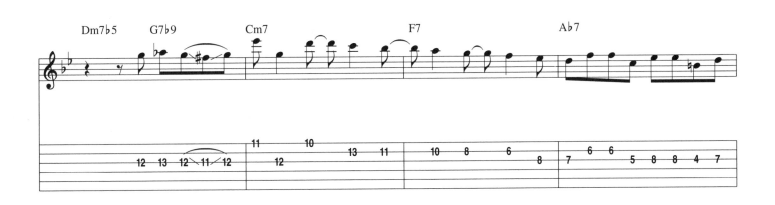

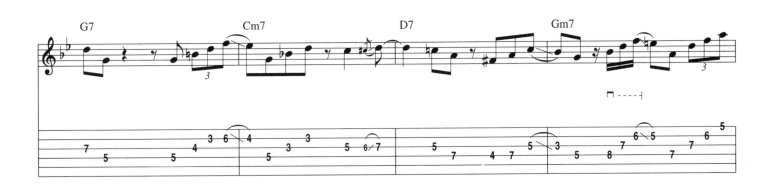

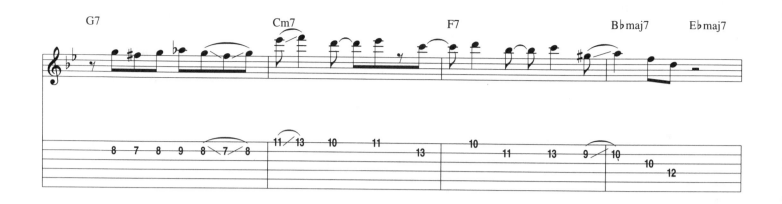

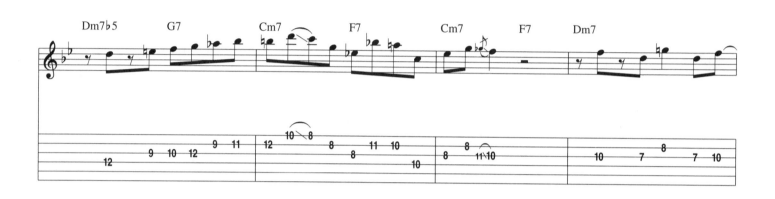

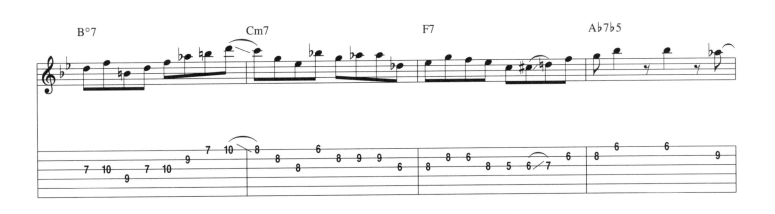

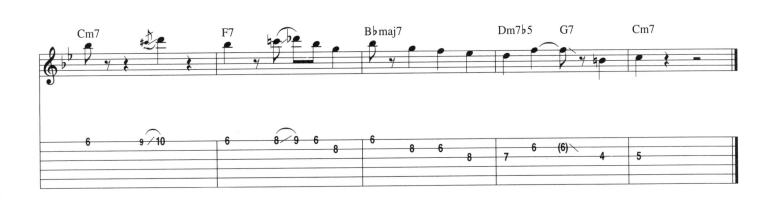

from SWING TIME

The Way You Look Tonight

Words by Dorothy Fields
Music by Jerome Kern

Copyright © 1936 Aldi Music and Universal - PolyGram Internatonal Publishing, Inc.
Copyright Renewed
All Rights for Aldi Music Administered by The Songwriters Guild Of America
International Copyright Secured   All Rights Reserved

* Played behind the beat.

* Guitar, drums and organ exchange four meas. solos ("trade fours") throughout section.

When Sunny Gets Blue

Lyric by Jack Segal
Music by Marvin Fisher

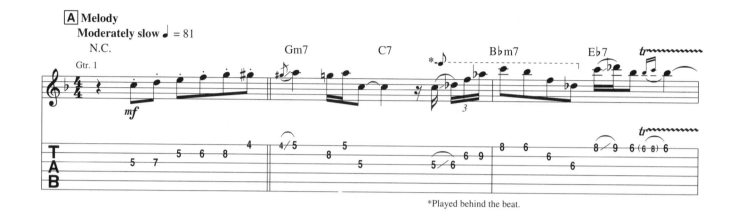

*Played behind the beat.

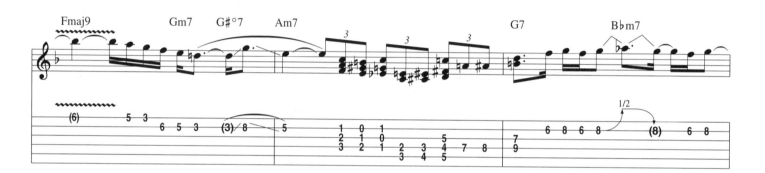

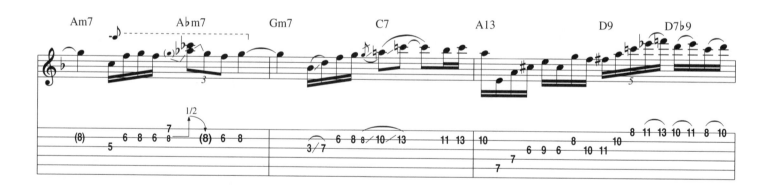

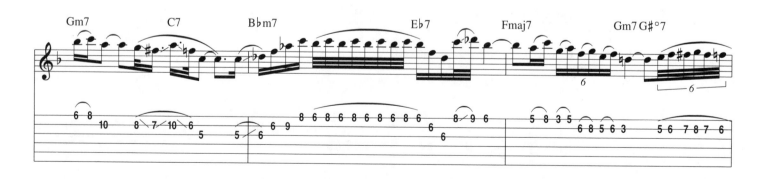

Copyright © 1956 Sony/ATV Tunes LLC
Copyright Renewed
All Rights Administered by Sony/ATV Music Publishing, 8 Music Square West, Nashville, TN 37203
International Copyright Secured   All Rights Reserved

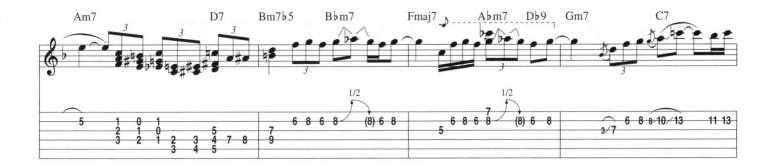

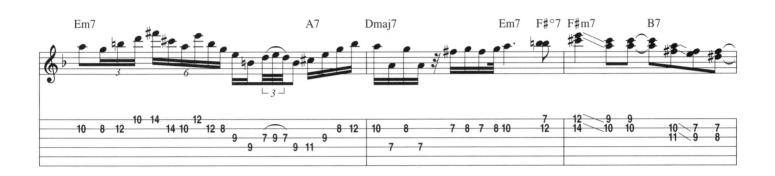

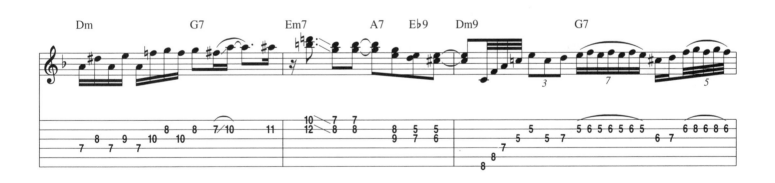

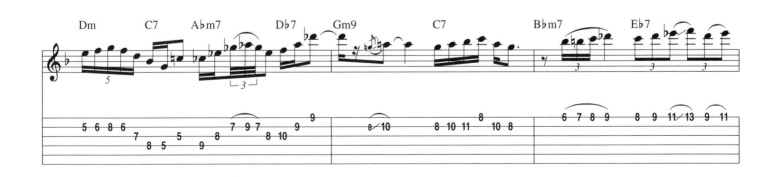

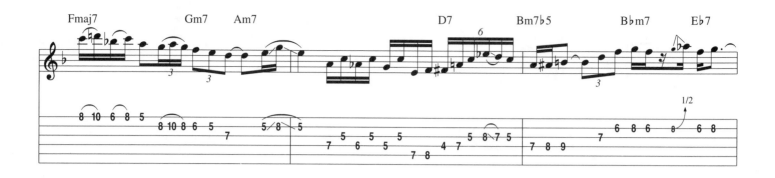

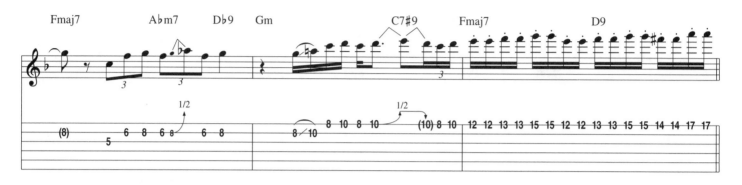

B **Guitar Solo**

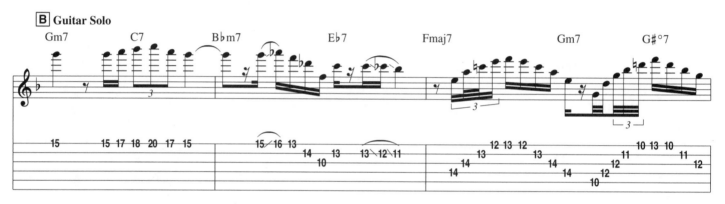

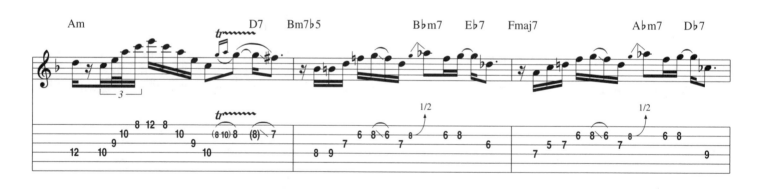

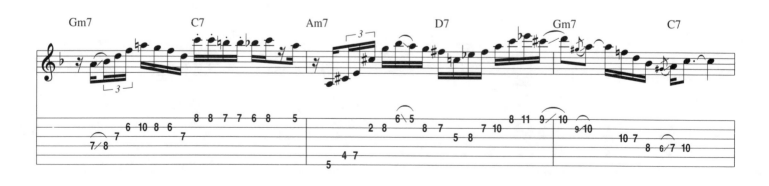

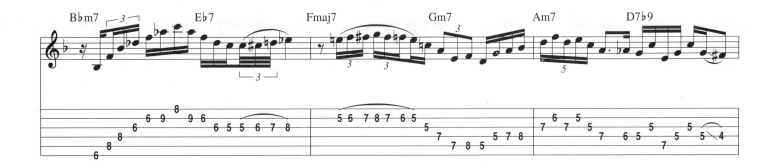

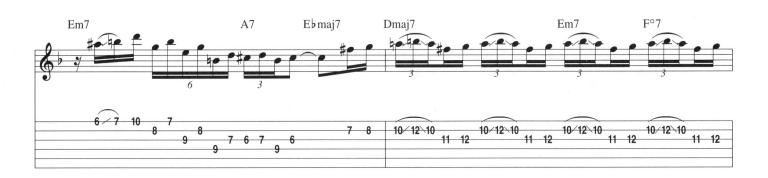

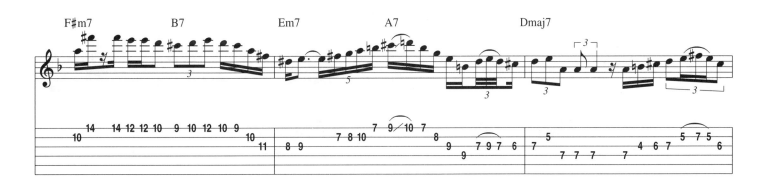

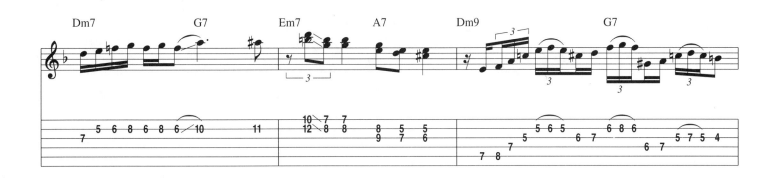

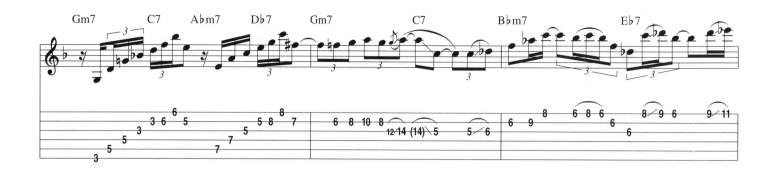

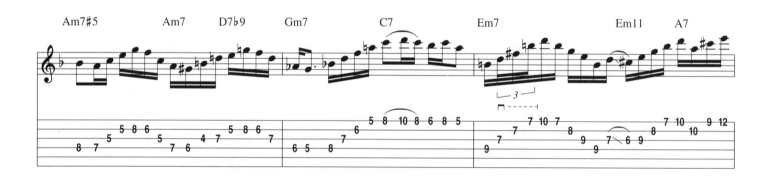

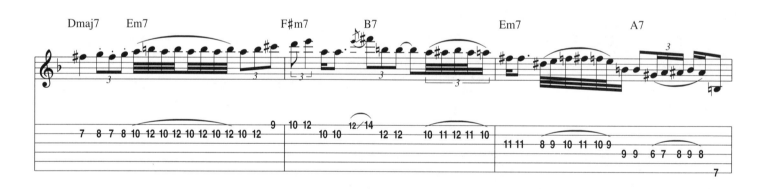

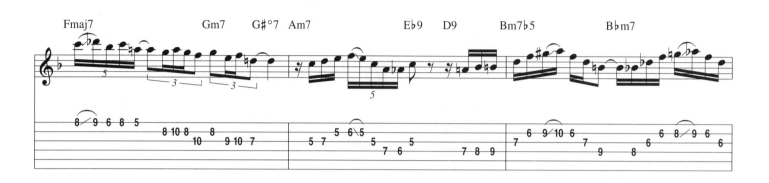

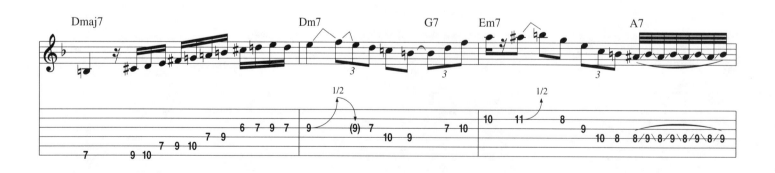

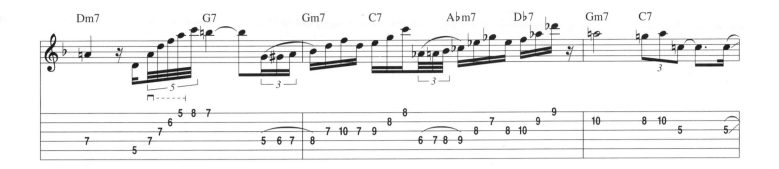

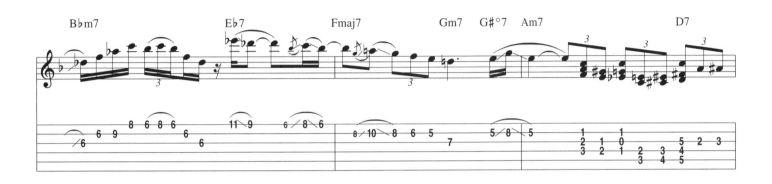

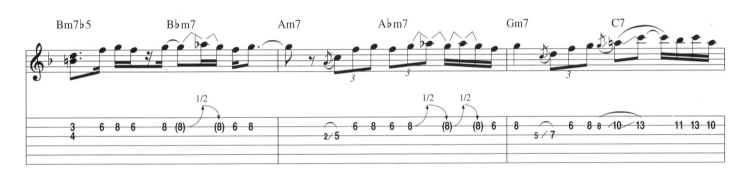

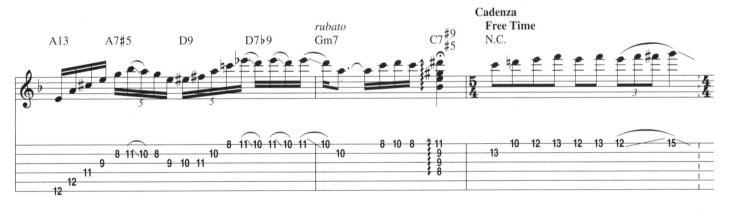

Guitar Notation Legend

Guitar Music can be notated three different ways: on a *musical staff*, in *tablature*, and in *rhythm slashes*.

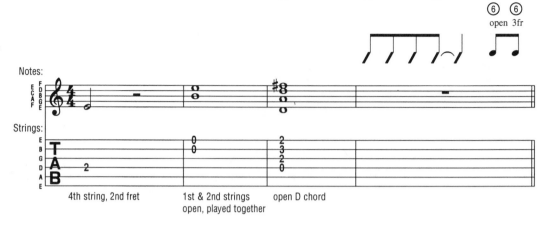

RHYTHM SLASHES are written above the staff. Strum chords in the rhythm indicated. Use the chord diagrams found at the top of the first page of the transcription for the appropriate chord voicings. Round noteheads indicate single notes.

THE MUSICAL STAFF shows pitches and rhythms and is divided by bar lines into measures. Pitches are named after the first seven letters of the alphabet.

TABLATURE graphically represents the guitar fingerboard. Each horizontal line represents a a string, and each number represents a fret.

4th string, 2nd fret

1st & 2nd strings open, played together

open D chord

Definitions for Special Guitar Notation

HALF-STEP BEND: Strike the note and bend up 1/2 step.

WHOLE-STEP BEND: Strike the note and bend up one step.

GRACE NOTE BEND: Strike the note and bend up as indicated. The first note does not take up any time.

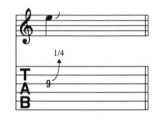

SLIGHT (MICROTONE) BEND: Strike the note and bend up 1/4 step.

BEND AND RELEASE: Strike the note and bend up as indicated, then release back to the original note. Only the first note is struck.

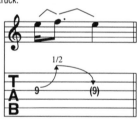

PRE-BEND: Bend the note as indicated, then strike it.

PRE-BEND AND RELEASE: Bend the note as indicated. Strike it and release the bend back to the original note.

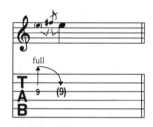

UNISON BEND: Strike the two notes simultaneously and bend the lower note up to the pitch of the higher.

VIBRATO: The string is vibrated by rapidly bending and releasing the note with the fretting hand.

WIDE VIBRATO: The pitch is varied to a greater degree by vibrating with the fretting hand.

HAMMER-ON: Strike the first (lower) note with one finger, then sound the higher note (on the same string) with another finger by fretting it without picking.

PULL-OFF: Place both fingers on the notes to be sounded. Strike the first note and without picking, pull the finger off to sound the second (lower) note.

LEGATO SLIDE: Strike the first note and then slide the same fret-hand finger up or down to the second note. The second note is not struck.

SHIFT SLIDE: Same as legato slide, except the second note is struck.

TRILL: Very rapidly alternate between the notes indicated by continuously hammering on and pulling off.

TAPPING: Hammer ("tap") the fret indicated with the pick-hand index or middle finger and pull off to the note fretted by the fret hand.

NATURAL HARMONIC: Strike the note while the fret-hand lightly touches the string directly over the fret indicated.

Harm.

PINCH HARMONIC: The note is fretted normally and a harmonic is produced by adding the edge of the thumb or the tip of the index finger of the pick hand to the normal pick attack.

P.H.

HARP HARMONIC: The note is fretted normally and a harmonic is produced by gently resting the pick hand's index finger directly above the indicated fret (in parentheses) while the pick hand's thumb or pick assists by plucking the appropriate string.

H.H.

PICK SCRAPE: The edge of the pick is rubbed down (or up) the string, producing a scratchy sound.

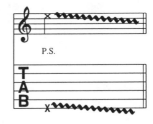

P.S.

MUFFLED STRINGS: A percussive sound is produced by laying the fret hand across the string(s) without depressing, and striking them with the pick hand.

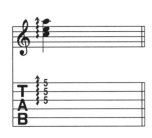

PALM MUTING: The note is partially muted by the pick hand lightly touching the string(s) just before the bridge.

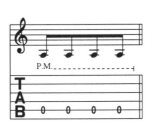

P.M.

RAKE: Drag the pick across the strings indicated with a single motion.

rake

TREMOLO PICKING: The note is picked as rapidly and continuously as possible.

ARPEGGIATE: Play the notes of the chord indicated by quickly rolling them from bottom to top.

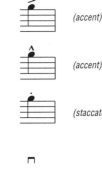

VIBRATO BAR DIVE AND RETURN: The pitch of the note or chord is dropped a specified number of steps (in rhythm) then returned to the original pitch.

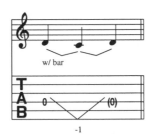

w/ bar

VIBRATO BAR SCOOP: Depress the bar just before striking the note, then quickly release the bar.

w/ bar

VIBRATO BAR DIP: Strike the note and then immediately drop a specified number of steps, then release back to the original pitch.

w/ bar

Additional Musical Definitions

(accent) • Accentuate note (play it louder)

(accent) • Accentuate note with great intensity

(staccato) • Play the note short

 • Downstroke

V • Upstroke

D.S. al Coda • Go back to the sign (𝄋), then play until the measure marked "**To Coda**," then skip to the section labelled "**Coda**."

D.S. al Fine • Go back to the beginning of the song and play until the measure marked "**Fine**" (end).

Rhy. Fig. • Label used to recall a recurring accompaniment pattern (usually chordal).

Riff • Label used to recall composed, melodic lines (usually single notes) which recur.

Fill • Label used to identify a brief melodic figure which is to be inserted into the arrangement.

Rhy. Fill • A chordal version of a Fill.

tacet • Instrument is silent (drops out).

 • Repeat measures between signs.

1. 2. • When a repeated section has different endings, play the first ending only the first time and the second ending only the second time.

NOTE: Tablature numbers in parentheses mean:
1. The note is being sustained over a system (note in standard notation is tied), or
2. The note is sustained, but a new articulation (such as a hammer-on, pull-off, slide or vibrato begins, or
3. The note is a barely audible "ghost" note (note in standard notation is also in parentheses).

PLAY LIKE THE PROS

Jazz Guitar Instruction

& Transcriptions

from Hal Leonard

The Jazz Style Of Tal Farlow
THE ELEMENTS OF BEBOP GUITAR
by Steve Rochinski

Finally, the book that defines the melodic and harmonic thinking behind the style of one of the most influential jazz guitarists of the 20th century, Tal Farlow. Includes instruction on: creating single-line solos; visualizing the neck; use of anticipation, expansion, and contraction; reharmonization; signature and chord voicings; chord-melody concepts; special signature effects such as bongos and harmonics; tune and solo transcriptions; and more!

00673245...$19.95

50 Essential Bebop Heads Arranged For Guitar

The best lines of Charlie Parker, Dizzy Gillespie, Thelonius Monk, and many more, for guitar with notes and tab. Includes: Donna Lee • Groovin' High • Ornithology • Confirmation • Epistrophy • and more.

00698990 ....$14.95

Jazz Guitar Chord Melodies
FOR SOLO GUITAR
arranged & performed by Dan Towey

This book/CD pack offers performance level chord-melody arrangements of 12 popular jazz songs for the solo guitarist. They range in difficulty from intermediate to advanced and include notes and tab. The CD includes complete solo performances. Songs include: All the Things You Are • Body and Soul • My Romance • How Insensitive • My One and Only Love • and more.

00698988 Book/CD Pack..................................$19.95

Chord Melody Standards for Guitar

15 great songs, including: Autumn in New York • Cheek to Cheek • Easy Living • Georgia on My Mind • The Girl from Ipanema • Have You Met Miss Jones? • Isn't It Romantic? • Stella by Starlight • The Way You Look Tonight • When I Fall in Love • When Sunny Gets Blue • more.

00699128...$9.95

Solo Jazz Guitar

The book starts with 11 lessons on chord melody concepts, then uses 20 familiar jazz standards to demonstrate these techniques, covering: diatonic and minor third substitution, contrary motion, back cycles, walking bass lines, modal chord scales, and more. Songs (in standard notation & TAB) include: All the Things You Are • Cherokee • Giant Steps • I Could Write a Book • Like Someone in Love • My Romance • Yesterdays • more.

00695317...$9.95

Best of Jazz Guitar
by Wolf Marshall
Signature Licks

Wolf Marshall provides a hands-on analysis of 10 of the most frequently played tunes in the jazz genre, as played by the leading guitarists of all time. Features: "St. Thomas" performed by Jim Hall, Tal Farlow and Kenny Burrell • "All Blues" performed by George Benson, Kenny Burrell and Pat Martino • "Satin Doll" performed by Howard Roberts and Joe Pass • "I'll Remember April" performed by Johnny Smith and Grant Green • and more!

00795586 Book/CD Pack...........................$19.95

101 Must-Know Jazz Licks
by Wolf Marshall
Signature Licks

Now you can add authentic jazz feel and flavor to your playing! Here are 101 definitive licks, plus a demonstration CD, from every major jazz guitar style, neatly organized into easy-to-use categories. They're all here: swing and pre-bop, bebop, post-bop modern jazz, hard bop and cool jazz, modal jazz, soul jazz and postmodern jazz. Includes an introduction by Wolf Marshall, tips for using the book and CD, and a listing of suggested recordings.

00695433 Book/CD Pack...........................$14.95

Jazz Guitar Improvisation
by Sid Jacobs

Develop your solo skills with this comprehensive method which includes a CD with 99 full demonstration tracks. Topics covered include: common jazz phrases; applying scales and arpeggios; guide tones, non-chordal tones, fourths; and more. Includes standard notation and tablature.

00695128 Book/CD Pack...............................$17.95

Joe Pass Collection

12 songs transcribed, including: Blues for Basie • Blues for Hank • Cheek to Cheek • Dissonance #1 • Happy Holiday Blues • I Got Rhythm • In a Sentimental Mood • Pasta Blues • Satin Doll • The Song Is You • The Way You Look Tonight • Yardbird Suite.

00672353..$14.95

JAZZ GUITAR GREATS

Learn the best lines of the masters! Each book/CD pack includes note-for-note legendary jazz performances transcribed and performed by Jack Grassel. The CD features two versions of each song at different tempos, with the rhythm section on a different channel. Includes standard notation and tablature.

Jazz Guitar Classics
Includes: Satin Doll/Kenny Burrell • Tangerine/Jimmy Raney • Honeysuckle Rose/Django Reinhardt • Billie's Bounce/George Benson • Stella by Starlight/Tal Farlow • Easy Living/Johnny Smith.
00698998 Book/CD Pack.................................$19.95

Jazz Guitar Favorites
Includes: All the Things That You Are/Hank Garland • I Hear a Symphony/Howard Roberts • Oleo/Pat Martino • Speak Low/Barney Kessel • When Sunny Gets Blue/George Barnes • Yesterdays/Wes Montgomery.
00698999 Book/CD Pack.................................$19.95

Jazz Guitar Standards
Includes: Falling in Love With You/Grant Green • I've Got You Under My Skin/Jim Hall • A Night in Tunisia/Billy Bauer • Stompin' at the Savoy/Charlie Christian • Yardbird Suite/Joe Pass • You Brought a New Kind of Love to Me/Chunk Wayne.
00672356 Book/CD Pack.................................$19.95

FOR MORE INFORMATION, SEE YOUR LOCAL MUSIC DEALER, OR WRITE TO:

HAL•LEONARD CORPORATION
7777 W. BLUEMOUND RD. P.O. BOX 13819 MILWAUKEE, WI 53213

www.halleonard.com

Prices, contents and availability subject to change without notice.

0800